How To Find Missing Persons. And Collect All Rewards Offers. The Formula.

THE CASE OF MADELEINE McCANN

David Gomadza

www.twofuture.world

DEDICATION

A better tomorrow.

CONTENTS

ACKNOWLEDGMENTS

A big thanks to Tomorrow's World Order

HOW TO FIND MISSING PERSONS AND COLLECT ALL REWARD OFFERS. THE FORMULA. THE CASE OF MADELEINE MCCANN

What happens when a person fails to show up home is critical do we call the police or wait to find out if not then what this is critical as you will see that humans procrastinate when it comes to finding people what happens to people when they disappear can be anything from being hit and run by a car or getting killed in a robbery that goes wrong now let's see what the brain says about disappearing people to know what happens we need case study and we can look at the case of Madeleine McCann case where she disappeared long time ago what happened that day was something from a movie script that even you will not believe that something like this will happen to a little girl like Madeleine now let's put the characters in place but this is exactly what happened on that day according to Yahweh time brain scan of all people involved now let's look at the facts Madel [short for Madeleine] was watching cartoons when there was a knock at the door and when she opened the door a man whisked her from the ground and into his arms and then signaled to the other in the car instantly a car drove fast to the gate outside the house and the girl was showed inside the car before the car drove off mean while Jerry Madel's father was watching television in the other room when he heard the screeching of car tires and instantly the car passed near his hotel bedroom window being driven fast he quickly got up and checked his hotel flat before heading out of the hotel into a caravan like hotel outside where Madel was with her mother at the time of abduction but she was asleep when this happened instantly he knocked the door and pushed it hard just before she woke up Kate [Madeleine's Mother] had just woke up after the commotion now fully shake did not know what had even happened until the husband said something drove really past the house as if a kidnap had just happened instantly she said where is Madel she felt lost and search the other room but the door was open and she was not inside that means that Jerry had felt the truth but how would he say exactly what had just happened without knowing something like sorry darling I fucked the baby when you were asleep now let's look at this case even deeper Jerry was easily aroused [looking at brain scans] by looking at his daughter when she was a little girl then he started watching her mother when according to him she sits like a man with a hard on leaning to the side now as time passed by Jerry would ask Madeleine to sit like mummy and then watch porn later but only adult pork if we Ask his brain this is the reply he could see her while watching older women

Now as time goes by he would ask his wife to dress like model but she would laugh and say how come Jerry when I have balls of steel to burn the jika meaning the hole in his arse meaning ask him to go to heaven using a code she had acquired as a doctor to kill her husband when she suspected he was cheating on her but she thought with her sister [arms] the code is 82987648689078582680 open wider Jerry but your own daughter you silly sititttt meaning shit-fuck-anus-with-leprosdick] Now Jerry would ask her to open wide her vagina but would turn her and do her in the butthole but she would cry at night every time he [lock forever send keys to asarsttrstssytytsurstuvwxyz] Now if Jerry wanted sex he would ask about his daughter first so that she opens wide but everytime he asks about the daughter she would perform to impress him squirting all over [faked using code 82987658432109826410] [let me squirte now lord of the heavens to protect my daughter from this sittitttt man with brain of a dick literally] Now what can be of Jerry this is the answer Jerry he was a plastic surgeon who asked for a replacement for his own penis with a prostrate one to please his wife but then everything stopped working until arousal started coming from his daughter [nhs code 98348567890982876851098285168l] Now what can be of nhs this is the answer nhs have used their knowledge to trap a couple into giving them coverage on the disappearance of their daughter to cover up everything and 87986584210 was responsible for the cover up but why [was the one fucking their daughter during routine training sessions to be a model] but also because of a 500 000 cheque received from UTC for coverage on the disappearance of Madeleine now Ask why UTC this is a channel for adults who abuse their own children and pocket the proceeds when they get them kidnapped but still it does not make any sense until you ask the brain why UTC then the answer is that because UTC is also the kidnapper and hidden of the child so that for years if not decades the child will not be found now let's Ask why madeleine then the answer is that Jerry could only get it up when she was there so removing her would render Jerry useless to Kate so that Kate can concentrate on helping people therefore become more productive to her employer [nhs] Now if we Ask why nhs this is because the couple had a take home of 7890000 per annum from the nhs this was highlighted often by the nhs managers now let's see why nhs might have been behind everything from the word go nhs was responsible for patients that the couple looked after as doctors having met at the university now in their late thirties nhs considered them unproductive because they made love 8 times per day in their office and the managers would spy on them using 78986848386776890285180 which is a spying device used in hospital office by nhs managers without consent and notice now Jerry had realized that they were being watched while at it and so would do it deliberately so that they raise the issue but waiting to sue them using invasion of privacy act of 1988 section 6 that prohibits unauthorized invasion of privacy now as they intensified their romps so that the managers complain nhs started switching Enzyme 1 of Jerry with Enzyme 2 where Enzyme 1 is male's for testosterone and Enzyme 2 is female's progesterone now if this happens Jerry would go for weeks without thinking much about sex now if we Ask why this is the answer so that he becomes productive for all that money they paid them now let's look the link between nhs and UTC UTC stands for United Telecommunication Company based in Australia but with subsidiaries globally if they were in England they would have been given contracts by the government but to cover nhs but they were in Portugal but for unknown reasons were paid by the uk nhs see record 789865872809238486721098489807620192816784849820 now this record shows that at the time of the disappearance of Madeleine nhs paid UTC 7.9286571580 in bitcoin which is equivalent of 56.9824000 Portuguese money equivalent to US$7.2 million the reason is not disclosed but if we Ask the brain this is the answer The bitcoin would cover her stay until 2026 when we get Jerry arrested for pushing his own daughter to the gangs by taking her there and tell his wife to keep her away from him if she doesn't want sex with him but all this is done to cover for nhs who used code 9876982845828094567890012348670284 to incapacity Jerry not just sexually but mentally by asking his wife to have sex with junior doctor [M] who first got the grip of it and refused outright but on a drunken night funded by nhs they made love for the first time and made Jerry listen through the spying instrument mentioned above so that if he sues them they can then say he was the first to use it to spy on his wife and they planned to incapacitate mentally during trials using nhs code 7744889678586 now what I have illustrated is the fact that even though Jerry and Kate were involved in their child's disappearance they were being blackmailed and tampered with by nhs managers using nhs codes to force them to do what nhs wanted meaning that they are victims and to some extend need the protection as well of courts to protect them against a clever but manipulating nhs who would not stop at anything now if we look at any laws they can use to make nhs managers pay as well there are 8 laws they can adopt to force the courts to apportion blame but if you read until the end nhs are the ones...

1. Forced redress there is a law that makes it illegal for people in a position of power to use weapons they have to make others do what they want especially if that involves forcing their families to act the way they did they can ask for maximum sentence which is dead sentence to the manager even if he or she did not authorize it as long as it can be proved that it happened on his or her watch

2 Incompetence by NHS to protect its employees by actually tampering with life of its employees to gain more from their employers at the end you will find out that all this is being played so that there is a change in law by...now if we Ask what can be done in this situation as punishment is the fact that nhs must be held fully responsible for the kidnap and sexual assault of Madeleine even if they had nothing to do with this the managers at the time must be charged with sexual assault kidnapping false imprisonment and adaption and paying kidnappers using illegal money in bitcoin and sexually castration Jerry just wait to hear what happened after this Now let's look at other offenses

3 kidnap and rape of a minor now let's Ask how and why this is so then you will see that if the law was fair nhs must pay for what they are doing now that we can prove it nhs used Jerry to push for a law that was abandoned during the second world War that prevents managers from interfering with life out of work hours now let's Ask what is this law then you will see why nhs must be behind bars as well nhs used a law called don't interfere with employers lives out of work hours even if that impacts their work and performance this law was enacted in 1943 but failed to reach the law hands to be passed but somehow found its way in hospitals where nhs managers would site it occasionally that

means Jerry and Kate were chosen to justify the use of this abandoned law where they have sex so much that they literally live at work for sex according to their secret files [brain scan reads] Now let's see how nhs targeted these to push for this law after they had got Jerry arrested in 2025 and sent him to jail in 2026 as a predatory father who used his wife as bait to use his daughter as food for the bait but without intention to eat the food but the bait itself[Roe v UK nhs] [1976] Now what can be of this law if we Ask the brain this law rests upon the premises that Jerry cannot be classed as a pedophile because his intention is not to eat the food the daughter here but used the daughter as food for the bait which is his wife that means if the food was not there there was no way he could go for the bait that alone is predatory and requires a jail sentence that would see all nhs doctors who will be judges give him maximum sentence of 30 years in jail reduced to 18 of good service and this would give them enough time and coverage to enforce the above law using those cases to highlight the need to protect children from fathers like Jerry now let's look st how this would have turned on according to them they would have tipped nhs doctors about Jerry and Kate as sex predators who nearly raped their own daughter on a drunken night then pay in bitcoin kidnappers who would snatch their daughter and now rape her so that when she is recovered they would say they are talking about the kidnappers and not them this would raise suspicion on their activities so that an enquiry in their conduct at work would have been known now to make things worse now in the driver seat hoping to bargain for the invasion of privacy would admit spying on them only because of tips of wrong doing but then deny it when they are caught that they have sold their daughter using bitcoin account which is linked to Jerry's purchase of a prostrate penis this would further trigger why questions why Jerry would need a prostrate penis and what happened to his this would highlight abuse where they would threaten his wife with trying to kill him using nhs code 789838764832109828423156 [sittitttt] Now if we can check what would be the effect of this accusation it would be to accuse him of something more serious and admit that she tried to kill him to stop him from harming his own daughter that would also explain why he need a prostrate penis this would be the first hand-job [laugh] of the mother to protect her own child but the truth is that Jerry suffered at the hands of nhs bosses who saw his romps with his wife at work as a challenge to their authority and to punish him they organized Kate to keep asking for a bigger dick than Jerry's but keep saying I don't what another man this would drive him nuts so that as a prostrate doctor he would know that he can indeed increase his manhood length and then still function normally even better with additions like code 98765832248106798280 which they all believed was responsible for his high sex drive with his own beautiful wife but the truth is that Jerry was having sex at work with his boss a man to protect his daughter from doctor who was giving her lessons as a model at the age of 3 years the same doctor who was going to see that his dick is castrated so that in the end he would admit that he is the one who ordered this so as to protect his daughter now the end of the twists and turns let's look at real facts Now 1 Jerry got his penis castrated during penis enlargement by doctors A. Asrelt who operated on him to increase his manhood but heavily sedated him [as a way to couch him how to get his wife drunk in order to sexually abuse his own with his new big weapon [dick.his] Now let's look why another prostrate doctor would want his rival out of the way nhs used a Muslim doctor who is against gay men to give him a real reason why he would sleep with another man this man prayed to Allah to forgive him but protested he was doing the right thing God [wept when he heard his prayer but crashed his soul for deliberately cut another man's priceless manhood something he would never do until...] Now let's look what happened day of the operation the doctor [Asia doctor knelt down and heavily sedated Jerry 10 times the normal dosage and prayed to Allah prestige urstuvwxy ssttuuvwxyz rstuvwxyz amen [Hebrew equivalent] but then said Allah at the end that alone made me question his motive and checked again and it turns out that he is Jewish and his prayer was in real Hebrew and it means Yahweh can you help me fix this mess but I have no regret to what I am going to do. Shalom [Allah] amen if you are to hear this first time it sounded like Arabic but then the Hebrew translation gave his identity now we look at why the cover from Hebrew to Allah Jerry hated Jewish people for ignorance and for getting Jesus killed but the truth is that the same doctor had refused to solve a puzzle he had there had been a heated argument between the two Jerry had insisted that .ya was not message to God but a reference to a place in the brain no doctor had discovered yet but the Jewish doctor had insisted that .ya was the brains way of sending messages to Yahweh God the creator [of which I represent] the message is the brain's way of communicating with the creator the person who created this is how I am the only one in the world heaven

hell or earth who can write the full account of what happened ... now let us check why the Jewish doctor did what he did to Jerry he had deliberately removed his own penis and swapped it with a prostrate meaning useless the operation was to put a sliced open one on top of his own but this doctor to prove a point now that there is a God who receive messages and can read messages his bet is that he spoke in a language which no other human being on earth can speak only language known by Yahweh that means that if another human being can receive this message and be able to read it that would mean that there is a God who authorized this person to read his message and if he can say exactly what he said in Hebrew but correctly in English then it means that it's proof that even though God speaks in Hebrew he also understand English otherwise how could he translate in Hebrew from English or according to Yahweh from Hebrew to English if this person who if correct according to prophecy who is not Hebrew can read and understand Hebrew then that means that God can read English if that is the case then Jerry's accusation that God can speak English would be just in vain to deny the truth now this argument is slightly different from the ones we were discovering about the proof of God as this one centre's around the language God speaks rather than how he speaks if we Ask him why this is the answer white people think God speaks English only therefore is a God for the English only which he refutes now let's look at why he removed his penis at first the reason appeared muddled this doctor used a prophetic verb from proverbs 10 v29 that says that God shall castrate innocent people to proof that God is greater than just a language Now let's Ask why he would go to such lengths this is why if someone can read this letter on earth and report him for castration him because alone how could he even open his mouth because the truth will come out that down there the greatest fucker in hospitals has been silenced by a Jewish that would make him contemplate suicide which would benefit everyone but now if someone else can report what happened and his prayer that means that God understand English how could he tell this person what to say in English exactly what he said in Hebrew if this happens then God will be there and people can read the brain and that he can talk to God who he send the message using
send.ya.messageaboutcastratingjerry.mccainn.now.foreverholdpeace.astr ilt.ya.now.send
Now let's address first this thing with the language first God even if he

can't speak english he can understand human language the human body records each word in 8 different languages that means even if the language of the mouth is totally unknown the other six body languages will be the same and the body has a match body parts translating language in that if it is talking about vagina or penis that was castrated then the other body languages that refer to penis and castration would be the same now what can we say about humans doing evil things to be the first to help discover Yahweh Allah or God humans have resorted to doing really bad things to each other just to help proof that ghe brain send message to Yahweh using send.ya but all this is useless to love Yahweh is to find Yahweh Now let's look at other grounds to challenge the nhs

4 nhs can be challenged for interfering with something so personal like a person's sex organs changing enzymes 1 and 2 switch between women and men enzymes that can cause mood swings and violence now if we asked what can be done of nhs in this regard the person doing it can be arrested we can easily identify this person using our Electromagnetic Wave Number Identifier where all you need is to play our video on YouTube that will tell you the person's Electromagnetic Wave Number which is unique to this person only his acetate and ghost a number used by only God to identify all forms of life on earth in heaven and in all universe

https://youtu.be/Kp5T4bLQjUg?si=uFRAsFnQLA8sqDPM

Now once we get that person's number we can start proceedings against this person for it is like those who abuse others and walk away we can make sure that we bring these to justice

5 we can tell the courts exactly the codes they are using and get these tested to prove that they have the desired effect now can we tell who is doing who by name house number and kids? Yes now this is the next step we then enter the electromagnetic wave number into the Identify the person by name database of all Electromagnetic wave numbers now we can use this information to identify who is doing what exactly and record this and forward to the courts now what can we bring up against these people we can argue for invasion of privacy misuse of government separates making and use of lethal viruses [most are digital viruses] we can say that it's deliberate grievous bodily harm which carry up to 20 years in jail if serious harm is done willfully causing of castration to further agenda willful damage to sexual organs with hope that they cannot be caught as they are hidden that brings in hacking

charges
Now back to the climax of the story a Rollercoaster if we are to make a documentary this will be one of the most watched docs ever now let's Ask ourselves why Jerry and Kate McCann the question is that they were picked at random by the institute of law of UK in a ballot that was thrown at the institute of law by professor Zubecka who was responsible for the choosing of the people to help the law of the interfering with private life if that affects normal work now we can see that this is not a case of mistaken identify in actual fact they were chosen to play this Rollercoaster game with personal consequences are such horrific to contemplate that all this is the works of a human being on another human being Now let's look at what happened to the day of the kidnapping Jerry was asleep and he received a brain text message that said are you sleeping Jerry when your wife is being fucked using your own real penis okay never mind it's your anywhere oh how big it was but women are clever if they know you will leave them one day they get you castrated for open up code 66885852867198368567902 for a what they call peace of vagina its bad thing to have a big dick and wanting an even bigger one to use on your ...missbutt when missbutt is your boss paying your salary of 789486000 this is like paying a porn star which I refuse to do as your boss now that you lost your huge dick which I loved the most now with your big prostrate ones you might as well start paying me this money for now I will refuse anything even cuddle from you I still can't understand why you would trust a Jew after talking all this through especially after promising that you will leave Kate for me who pay you this kind of money for such a poor job if it was you operating we could have been sued out of money but you listened you better fuck the boss and let the Jew do the cutting but the Jew in the end used that experience to cut you I cried the way I never cried even when my wife died of cancer killed by nhs so that I work harder and more productive then there you are after warning you you go and try to please a bitch- any woman who say increase your dick size is not worth a thing for not listening and trusting me I walk out of your sittitttt life your wife will end you if not the hospital will I saved your life it was me who created antidote at a huge cost that saved your life that day you fainted the code your own wife sent you was supposed to paralyze you yet you stuck with her so go and pleasure her Now with useless prostrate penis Jerry I hate you for not loving me the way I loved you I feel hurt that I tried to kill myself using your wife's anti I

mean dose but I had taken anti as well you know how probably but inside I have been permanently damaged something fell out from my ass I wish it was my arse that I wished it was it that chopped your dick at least I would have started mending it back but...bye but I tell you this that you are now the most feared man in the hospital imagine threatening to sue hospital for illegally listening to your romps with your wife then the same hospital accidentally chopping your dick off surely that's prison sentence for the manager who happens to be your gay lover I will try again to kill myself but if not then you know the drill now I have to fuck your daughter I cried when nhs doctors told me what happened to you they both suspected sex with you so I said I was giving your daughter lessons and they said what lessons then I imagined thinking it sexually then being dragged to court before you [this will happen in the future on 28 February 2025] Now imagine the confusion that created that I teach your daughter who is only 3 years modeling I guess being an open gay helped me in that area but it's those things that happen when you are not prepared what to say now I must go bye and be careful they want to use your daughter to stressgume you before taking you to court for something to do with the disappearing of your daughter Jerry instantly fully woke up to him he felt scared about his daughter he actual asked himself if he is going to kill his daughter his acetate refused to answer saying if you get subpoenaed what happens to your acetate that flicked him that he asked his wife to keep his daughter away from him and to watch her all the time and him especially when he is asleep Jerry the day they went abroad after refusing several times was a stressful day that afterwards he came back and slept his wife all this time was crying for his dick the reason why she married him Jerry had a big dick according to all his women and gay lovers but he never believed so or became possessed with size mostly the thickness rather than the shaft this day she had begged him to fuck her with the prostrate one with the help of his hand it was 8 weeks without sex that she started threatening him to see Asrelt the man who had castrated him this paralyzed him with fear than he would inject himself with sleeping morphine to sleep from the trauma now let's look at Kate herself to understand her motives Kate had a rough upbringing where her father would look at her sexually but never touched her but would run and fuck her mother over the years she had resented this when Jerry found out she used to like it Jerry out of stupidity after joking to choke Kate with his duck decided to increase the roundness by adding a dead person's sliced dick on top of his so that when he get aroused his gets huge and the dead persons expands with blood making everything look cumbersome all this to make his wife cum for she had confessed that because of seeing her father naked like that looking like he had another dick on top of his she could not orgasm and had never orgasm despite being a doctor and Jerry had joking decided make his look like her father's then remove that childhood trauma with her own husband she had partly agreed but had refused for operation she had actually purchased a fake one that looked like that with another on top of it after a friend had one made on her 28 birthday now Jerry this day woke up late and started to read her diary she had never left behind before now this is the interesting party after Jerry had suggested having his put a top she had the same say asked Asrelt the Jew surgeon for a date stripping all her clothes for him but had cried and said my daughter no not you I want to fund your mother with disease why you need disease you are young from now on say no I don't want fungus now soon after she had walked out of his office without any clothes just before another person entered in but without seeing her but all this being watched by the jealous manager now later the manager goes into Asrelt office and also removed all his clothes and stood to see what Asrelt would do but he threw a tantrum later that day now what happened after this was out of this world for Kate ever since they got married she had never masturbated that much or beg anyone else for sex this day what had happened with Asrelt was that she had gone in his office an asked him direct for fuck once just to enjoy sex with a sheikh [Shalom] but the Shalom had refused saying he can only have sex with his wife alone who he loved greatly to even consider her but asked why he hears sex all the time in her husband office exactly same time but just before he finished talking he started hearing the talking of two people as the volume becomes audible he realized Jerry's voice but with a male so he relaxed and started writing his notes then he started hearing the moans but assumed it was now with Kate and instantly his door opened up and Kate stood in his office then instantly as the moans stopped in her husband's office she removed all her clothes and stood in front of Asrelt who kissed her on the forehead and treated her like his own daughter and really slapped her hard that she cried like a girl and run out of his office naked but came back and took her own clothes and said it's too big that's the only reason I cry if it was like yours why would I cry and not cum Asrelt cursed and lifted his hands to slap her again but took out his own dick and forced her down and said big or small its not yours look I removed my own for you so you enjoy sex with prostrate like your father and your mother after you left home now if you don't want to come either go away with her or sell her instead there is no man out there who would remove his penis because my daughter who I never touched can't accept who I am so I refuse this time sell that tight brat I can't cut prostrate for you again nothing works anymore even the prostrate now you go and find men who look like women and give your daughter to them go fuck hell out of my life daddy has a big thing hanging I never showed her my dick so go away this time maybe I kill her myself in my sleep I am scared okay you go Kate looked confused because it was Asrelt taking and not Jerry when she opened the door to go he grabbed her by the waist and cried profusely saying; I love you Kate I love you Madele I love you Kate and I love you smalltight like your daughter only that it's on you clever nhs it's not my dick that's big it's your vagina that's small too small to enter even at the door this is not life so let's start fuckin hard my smalltighttightghtghttight

stop it its you shrinking it so you have grounds to have sex with Asrelt Asrelt did as if he had just woken up from a command the message about Jerry thinking of having gay sex with him a Jew caused a huge lump in his throat that he nearly stabbed on his return from the other office but she had worn her clothes and ran out instantly Ajert entered his office to find him swearing holding a big scissors like knife what's with you with knives like scissors Asrelt laughed so hard that he cried after that but to his surprised Ajert just left without a word sorry Jerry I missed she ran quickly that means she is not abused by you otherwise she could have stopped thinking for me to attack her you are a free man its not you not even your daughter nhs framing you but how... he sat down and asked his acetate

Why nhs wants to get Jerry arrested in 2025 to be specific on 24 August 2025?

Acetate took time to answer

Okay file retrieved nhs v Jerry for child molestation and getting her killed in the process

killed when this is not in the acetate system why

Ransom failed in 2024 September 26 why he sat down nhs never finish plan because they always get leaked by stupid fast acetate but will always reduce the time frame by exactly a quarter of that date from any

given date which will work out the same meaning on 26 September 2024 Madeleine is found dead by who?
Not dead but alive rescued and ...
Acetate laughed do you think If they told anyone then people would die? How many rescues you know seriously?
Hesitated none exactly zero nada penieto panta pula pulsk 0 that means no one beats acetates and no one can conquer acetate world we are the best but if we find God then we can win because we can reveal all your past to know all your future humans to find God is like finding my own balls in my small intestines not that I have intestine but in my imaginary ones [laugh]
A big knock at the door Jerry stood there holding his dick in his hand do you want to fuck this giant only you left now Asrelt the Jew with shit in the xxrrssttuvwxyz
Asrelt tightened the grip on his hand holding the scissor like knife I am ready but I am a professional I need an appointment let's say 3pm just death time
Okay 3pm it is oil properly Jews arse like a bush I do clean shave only so how was my wife's pussy I mean shaven pussy is she hot I refused to fuck a kid inside your wife why not take her out with exorcism or orgasm if you can maybe that 500 000 cheque for the synagogue will come at last now if you can help me clarify things here you refused sex with someone with a crush on you I said there is a kid inside your wife take the kid out first then I can do her your wife like adults like man to man boys to boys where are the boys nhs sorting the boys why i thought this is here was here but nhs refused no accident at the hospital thorough investigations will get us all caught up okay where?
Put his fake prostrate dick in his pocket and sighs that's my daughter fuck nhs I leave this job if she finds out when she is grown up I have to get this chopped fir an alibi her father was a doctor trapped by nhs I can't my life too precious for money I leave this job if it was for acetate mimicking everything I could have had sex with men but I have never just I thank my wife and acetate here shaking the prostrate dick you can say that he instantly said as I'd a robot has just spoke so what can we do? Go to Portugal lose her for years they will find her in 2024 September that means you must find her a quarter before that or she is dead for public stunt going wrong has anyone ever recovered?
Asked Jerry breathing hard yours will be the first go in peace Shalom remember I removed your penis that tells all that there was no sex

involved even if she dies go and sell her for how much again
They said 0.79 bitcoin or 7.92 bitcoin I can remember but remember
this if you talk she will die if you find her she will live so go and do her
and find her you know the drill you get paid in bitcoin nhs currency
Satoshi my arse acetate here is my witness when bitcoin nhs
June 28 2000
Now what do you need before you go I only ask as a friend I have
acetate to guide me through this sittitttt they both laughed how is Kate
coping with all this? Doing great but can be better if you ask me I know
it's going to be tough how can you pretend something like this has ever
or never happened why do we have to go through all this you were
chosen at random by Zackeb so fight till the end the law will be named
after you but if God was listening in he would simply expose all this
and get the law but for putting nhs shit its right full place away from
our kids I would vehemently testify that these are the shits spoiling our
kids and other races there was silence I thought you don't believe in
Yahweh someone in my shoes will believe anything to save family
speaking of which if I get caught up can you do her for me but with
your huge hands cut her slowly out okay [silence,]
You are asking me to do your wife?
Only if found alive if dead then do me out okay
Okay
Now if we look at all this conversation you will see that they are
actually cutting deals with nhs staff [managers] who organize these
publicity deals but where women and children are the real victims all
this because there is no man or woman who could put all this together
to know exactly what goes on in the brain until now ladies and
gentlemen now I reveal the real culprits behind all this and all this for a
loaf of bread these are the organizers of the faked or forced abduction
1 corporal segment St Mary's
2 Corporal Segement Doughty
3 nhs London headquarters
4 nhs headquarters
5 nhs haul
6 nhs leeds Bradford
7 nhs somerset
8 nhs default
9 UTC
10 jerry mcCann

11 Kate mccann
12 Asrelt
13 Assert CPU
14 Ajert
15 Art
16 Ast
17 Ajt
18 Adt
19 Azt
20 Adst
21 Dest
22 Desst
23 Desst
24 Dessttuv
25 Sstuv
26 Jsml
27 Jjttuv
28 Astuv
29 Ajst
30 Numset
31 Dusetmnop
32 Destuv
33 pptuv
34 Ppnt
35 Zzstt
Now Ask why we must bring all nhs staff to justice?
They are the ones organizing these drills that brings all players together
so they all have a job and where all selected people die no one has ever
been served that means 100 per cent death rate sp that no one can
report them but Yahweh has arisen among us so fear not children and
women the might shall fall this springs so who must be dragged to
court and why and when
1. Pc Shortly
2 Pc Stuvwerty
3. Pc Mnopqrst
4 Pc Xztomnop
5 Pc Xtoprmnopqrs
6 Pc 789865
7 Pc Smiterty

8 Pc Zerf
Now Ask why?
These had an opportunity to oppose nhs but decide to refuse and take promotion instead some were paid in kind with nhs prostitutes etc.
Now we look at the charges against the McCann
1 neglecting their own child where they knew exactly what to do and where to report nhs
2 assaulting their own daughter for a loaf of bread [roughen her up]
3 making up storied to facilitate nhs to do harm to their child
4 to add to this list is Pc Steven's who stopped the thieves with the girl on road in Portugal before escaping to Spain to Rosti City 28389876542310086923400 North of Cansas Portugal
Now this is Madeleine's electromagnetic wave number 76892832290786458321099865421 56
Now how do we find exact location?
You simply use our Electromagnetic Wae Digital Analogue alerter on YouTube
Electromagnetic Wave Digital Identifer
https://youtu.be/b90bVm8sNng?si=OtlKWXZK6EfO5UOR
Now just what you want to know
1. The name pf the person
2. The phone number
3 the Electronagnetic Wave Number
4 Home Address
5 Wireless WiFi
6 GPS tracker code
7 Positive Identifier
8 Vocals for voice pattern
9 ASAP Associated Supposed As Person's on that day
10 Voice recognition serial number
Now add a Thoughts to words or Audio and get what they were thinking at the time of the crime
Ladies and gentlemen this is how Tomorrow's World Order are to look for missing persons

Visit www.twofuture.world
Signed
08May 2024
David Gomadza

07719210295
Davidgomadza@hotmail.com
Info@twofuture.world
United Kingdom

OUR MISSING PERSONS SEARCHING TOOLS LINKS

Digital Identifier phone number, address. Electromagnetic Wave Number etc

https://youtu.be/b90bVm8sNng?si=wE1l3zTdxtvNLKpQ

The Electromagnetic wave number Identifier Assigner Digital Analogue

https://youtu.be/f3hgj7sCaIs?si=hPF1UjqR2HdEG5bd

A Digital Thoughts To Words Converter
https://youtu.be/i5KCRpKqmqY?si=l7X6waiBHNngAgw9

All our missing persons searching tools;

ABOUT DAVID GOMADZA

David Gomadza
www.twofuture.world